How to Convert a Book to Epub Format
Let Smart Phone Users Pay to Read Your Book on Their Phones

Robert Rodgers PhD

Contents

Who Will Benefit from Creating Error Free Epubs?

Who will benefit from the information in this book? Have you published an existing book that is available in print form as a paperback or hardback and/or released an ebook for download to computers? If so, you will benefit handsomely if you have not yet converted your existing book files to epub formats. Without a conversion of your existing book files to an error free epub format, your books can not be read on smart phones. Until they are converted you will lose sales of your book from people

© Zero Point Healers

who prefer to read books on their smart phones.

Smart phones are the leading technology of the future. Few people will be using desktop or laptop computers to read books five years from now. Rather, most people will use smart phones to work, connect, email and read books. Convert your book to an epub format now to take advantage of an expanding market that will dominate book sales in the future.

Why Does My Book Need to be Converted to Epub Format?

OK. So you already have a clean, error free book file as a PDF or a doc file (a word file) which has been used to create your paperback and/or ebook. Why can't one or both of these files substitute for epubs? Why can't I just rename the file extension from .doc or .docx to .epub? It can't be that complicated, eh?

The problem in a nutshell is that the files you use to print your paperback book are

© Zero Point Healers

set for a large print space. Many books are 8.5 inches wide by 11 in height. Standard programming for books sets the width of pages to be wide.

Have you ever seen a phone that is 8 inches wide? All of the existing programming has to be changed to accommodate the small screen space that is available for viewing on phones, tablets and other devices.

Perhaps you are wondering why your PDF file can't simply be reduced in size? The print would be so small that no one would be able to read your book - including you. All in all, a significant conversion in programming is necessary to make your existing print book (or even ebooks which can be downloaded to computers) readable on phones.

The bottom line is this. If you want people in future years to read your books you will need to convert them to epubs or, alternatively, write them originally as epubs. I think the better process is to start with the paperback format which is subsequently converted to an epub format. This instructional book offers you the steps that must be taken to convert your existing book to an epub format.

Who Am I?

I am a former university professor at the University of Kentucky who quit a tenured position to write and publish without having to hassle with reviewers, editors and referees who would consistently demand that I water down my writing for the work to be accepted and published.

When I realized sales of my books were not increasing, I decided to convert them to epubs. More people were reading books on their smart phones than on their computers. Fewer people were reading my paperback books.

I searched and searched the internet and found little help and guidance. Believe me when I say that I spent days searching for the answers. The help that I did get was usually outdated. Many of the leads from the internet resources resulted in frustration and wasted energy. It took me two months to figure out how to do the conversion. Since I encountered so many obstacles and problems converting my own books I decided that what I had learned would be of immense benefit to others. All of the lessons learned are the inspiration for this book.

This book will explain what took me eight weeks to figure out. Follow the steps I outline below. In most cases you should be able to generate your epub in an hour or two or even less time. Trust me when I say the conversion will be worth the effort.

Really? Is it Really Worth the Trouble to Convert My Book to an Epub Format?

Answer is simple. You will increase sales of your books dramatically. If you do not care whether people read your books and have little interest in generating a reliable revenue stream every month then the answer is no. It will not be worth your trouble.

Why Won't One Simple Program Complete the Conversion?

Answer: You will probably not get them posted on Google Play because of errors.

How to Get the Most out of These Step by Step Instructions

Read each step of the conversion described below. Once you complete the step, move onto the next step. You cannot complete the steps in random order. Each step must be completed before proceeding to the next step of the conversion process.

I personally like to skip around when I work but this habit will slow you down and require extra effort to complete the conversion. Once you become familiar with the steps described next you will be able to convert your books in 5 -10 minutes.

© Zero Point Healers

Step One: Get the Best Extension for Your Book in Word

Below is a screen shot of 2010 Word. Of you have a Microsoft Word program that you used to write your book, activate it in your computer now. Click on "File" in the top left of the screen. Click "Save As." Then save to the selection "Word."

If you do not have Microsoft Word save your book to an HTML version if available. The best version is in a .docx format because it generates the fewest errors. A screen shot of Word is presented on the following page.

© Zero Point Healers

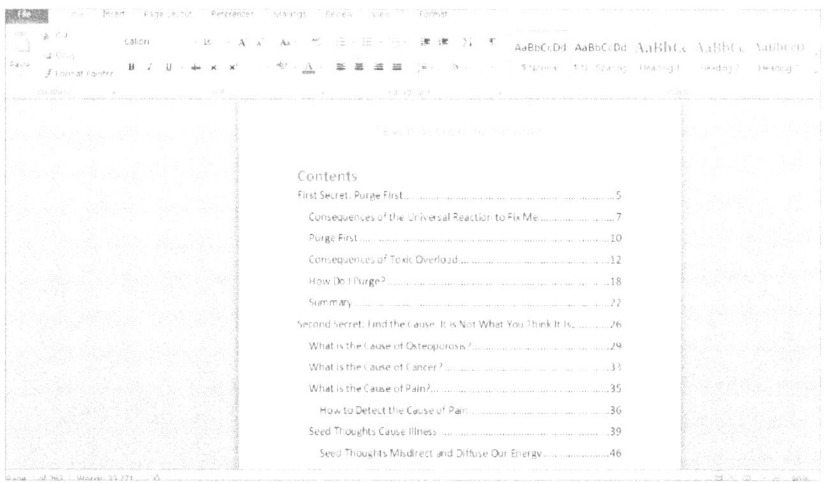

Step Two: Download Calibre (Free and Safe)

How to Download Calibre

Are you comfortable with downloading programs onto your computer?

Click on the link below to start the download. If the link flops, simply copy and paste the download link shown below into your browser to retrieve the Calibre download.

http://calibre-ebook.com

Sometimes you will click on the link above and you do not arrive at the download page as expected. Every computer works a bit differently.

© Zero Point Healers

If this happens, you will need to copy the link and paste it directly into your browser (whether Internet Explorer or Bing or Safari – or whatever search engine you use).

How do I Copy and Paste the Calibre Download Link?

1. Highlight the Calibre website address download link below.

    http://calibre-ebook.com

2. Press the button labeled Ctrl on your keyboard at the same time you press the letter c on your keyboard. Nothing will show up - but you will have just copied the download link that you highlighted. Make sure the entire link is highlighted before you copy it.

3. Bring up your search engine (whether internet explorer or Bing or Safari or …)

4. Place your cursor in the field found in the very top of your search engine which is where the actual addresses of websites appear. Erase whatever address pops up

© Zero Point Healers

(the field in your browser will begin with www. or http://www.)

5. Press the Ctrl button down again on your keyboard and this time press the letter v on your keyboard at the same time (not the letter c). The download link that you copied will now show up in the address field at the top of your browser where you placed your cursor. It is like doing magic!

This is the most expedient way to copy and paste anything. You can type the download link directly into the address field of your browser but it is easy to make mistakes with an address this complicated.

6. Press enter on your keyboard and you will be brought to the Calibre download page.

7. You will need to have the program saved on your computer since we will be using it in a few minutes. The download will automatically insert a Calibre icon on your desktop. When you get ready to use the program, click on the Calibre shortcut icon

on your desktop. When you do – you will see the Calibre page that looks like the screenshot below (without the listing of my books).

Step Three: Download Sigil (Free and Safe)

Click on the link below to start the download of Sigil. If the link flops, simply copy and paste the download link shown below into your browser. If you do not know how to copy and paste a link,

© Zero Point Healers

skip back to page 11 where you will find instructions.

http://www.download.cnet.com/sigil/3000-2341_4-75332057.html

After the download when you click on the Sigil icon on your desktop will look something like this:

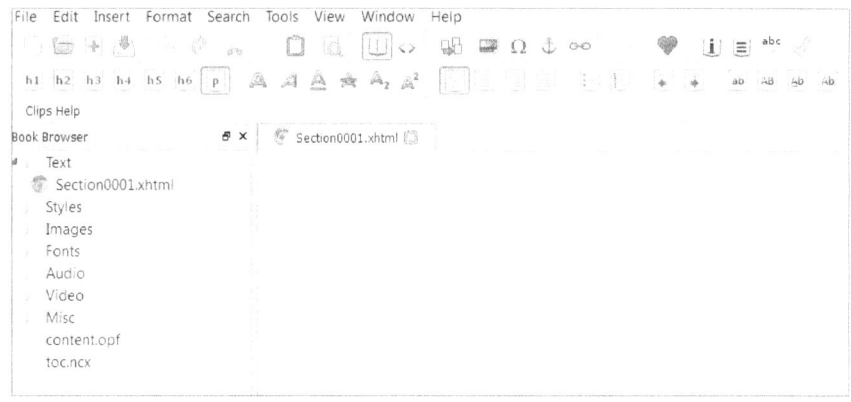

© Zero Point Healers

Step Four: Convert Your Book to an Epub Using Calibre

Bring up Calibre by clicking on the Calibre icon on your desktop. Clicking the icon activates the program to run on your computer. The page that comes up will look like the screen shot below (without the listing of books).

© Zero Point Healers

In the top left corner of the Calibre screen there is a red square that reads "Add Books." Click on that menu item and a drop down menu will appear.

Open your book into Calibre by clicking on the top selection of the drop down menu which reads "Add Books from a Single Directory." A dropdown menu will pop up asking you to select the book you wish to load from your computer. Select the book file saved in the folder on your computer with the extension you wish to convert to an epub (preferably with a .docx format or if not, in a web html format). Your book will be listed in the column titled "Title."

Click on the menu item at the top that reads "edit Metadata" which is listed below the blue circle with the letter "I" inside. This will bring you to a screen that shows the details of your book.

© Zero Point Healers

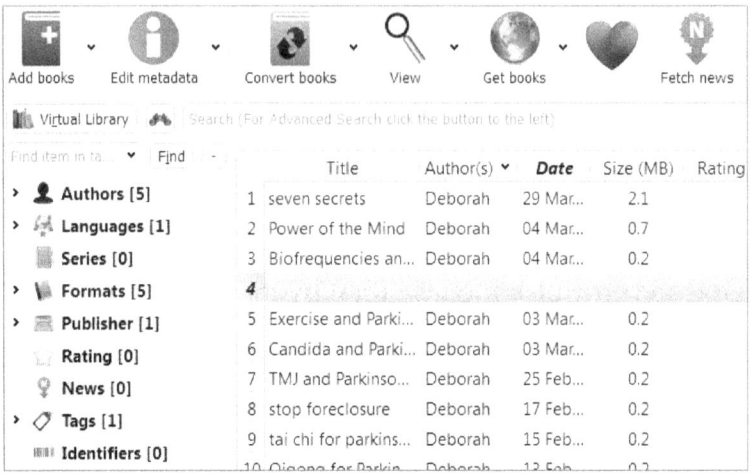

After clicking on Edit Metadata (see above) a panel looks like the screen shot below (with a book of my own displayed). Make sure the basic information is correct including the title and the file extension. Make any changes necessary.

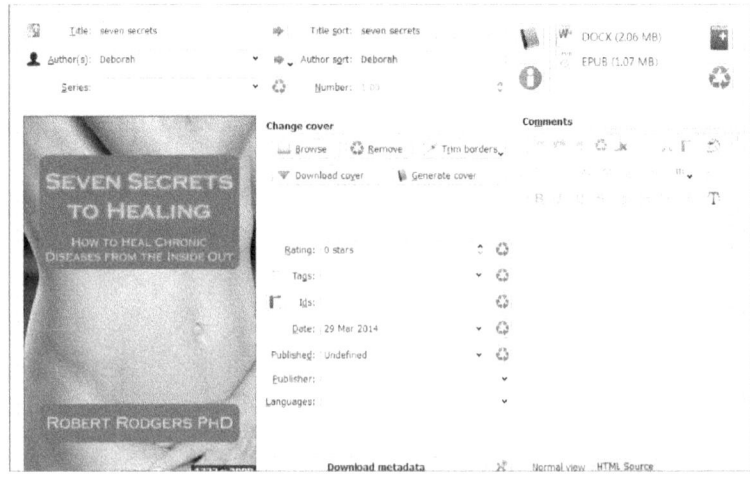

© Zero Point Healers

Delete the meta data screen by clicking on the "x" in the right top corner of this page. This will bring you back to the main Calibre screen.

Click on "look and Feel" highlighted in blue above. The screen above will pop up. Click on the selection in the middle of the panel titled "remove spacing between paragraphs." You will want to see a check mark beside this field as shown above in the screen shot. This is the only change you need to make to this screen. Click OK in the bottom right hand corner of the panel (not shown above).

Click on the sixth menu item down the list of menu items titled "Table of Contents." It is

© Zero Point Healers

highlighted in blue below. The panel below will show up. Now click on the icon to the right of the arrow above.

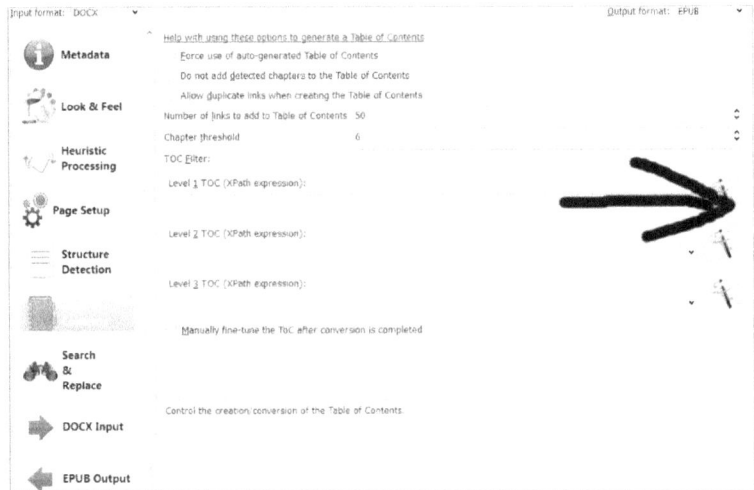

A menu will be displayed that is shown on the following page.

© Zero Point Healers

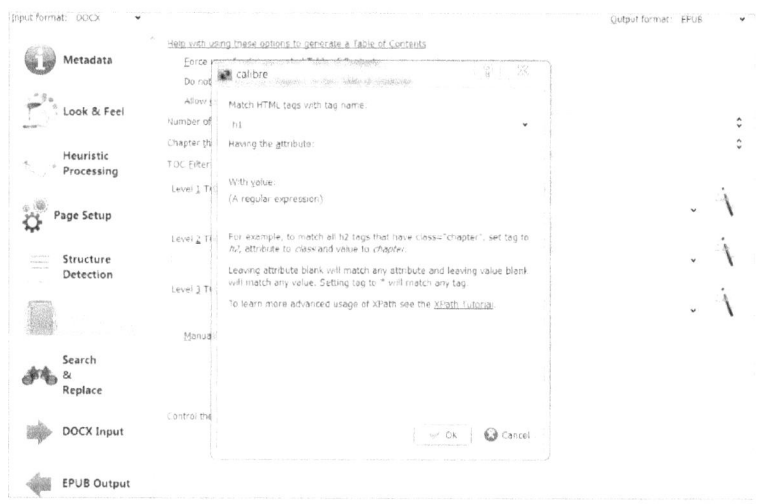

The field at the top of this drop menu is titled "Match HTML tags with Tag Name." Bring up the drop down menu by click on the arrow in the right of the field. Select h1 from the drop down menu. Then click OK in the right bottom corner.

As shown in the screen shot on the following page the field is automatically populated with //h:h1 after clicking OK. You do not have to do anything.

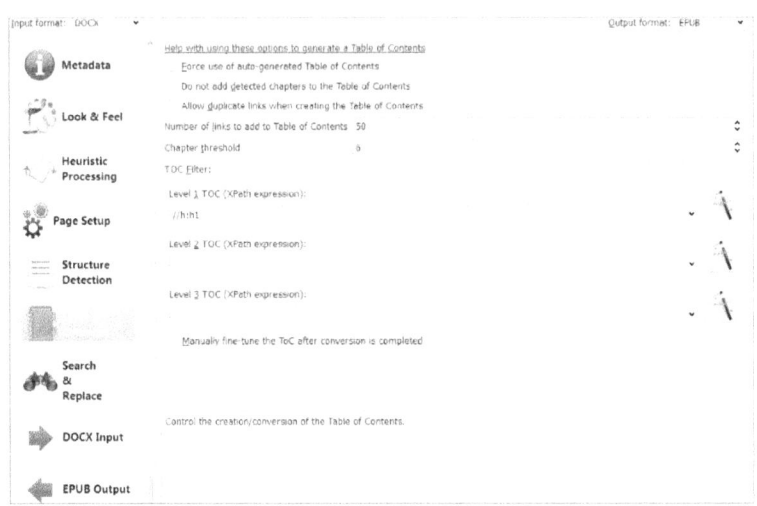

Without clicking anywhere else your epub file is being generated. You can view the progress by looking in the right bottom corner of the screen.

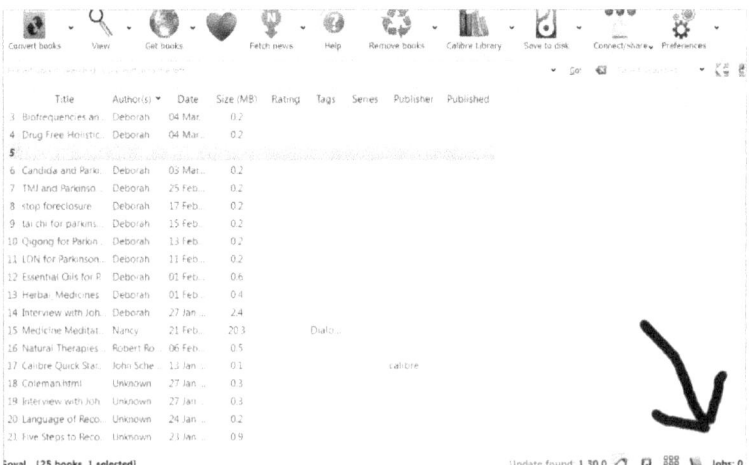

When "jobs" in the right hand bottom corner reads 1, the epub files are being built. When

© Zero Point Healers

"jobs" show 0, the creation has completed. This only takes about 10 seconds. You will receive no notice that the epub book has been built other than seeing the "jobs" in the bottom right corner display a 0 which means all jobs are complete.

The epub file itself is not listed anywhere on the panel. Don't worry. It is there! The next step is to save it to your computer.

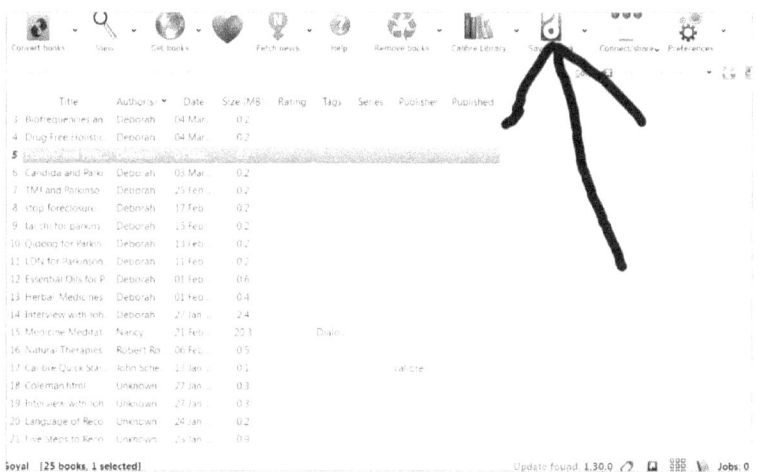

As shown above with the black arrow, click on the "save to disk" selection which is the first drop down menu choice. You then get to choose which folder on your computer you wish to save the epub file that has just been created.

© Zero Point Healers

A folder is required because more than one file will be saved. You may need to create a new folder for this purpose. Once you have selected the folder click save. All the files will be saved to that folder. The most frustrating part of the conversion can be that you may forget which folder the epub files have been saved. Make a special note to remember where you save them. You are now done with Calibe.

Step Five: Open the Epub file in Sigil for Editing and Correcting Errors

Part of you is probably thinking that if you already created the epub in Calibre – why bother to go any further? There are two reasons.

First, you will want to inspect the appearance of your book as an epub which is how people will read it on their phones and tablets. You will always need to edit the book a little to make its appearance look professional. Sigil is a basic epub editing program that can be used to clean up and edit your epub book.

© Zero Point Healers

Second, the conversion process often generates errors. You must fix these errors if you want to list and sell your book on Google Play or many of the other epub download services.

The next step is to use the Sigil program (that you have already downloaded) to edit your book and check for errors. Below is a screen shot of Sigil which will come up on your computer when you click the Sigil icon on your desk top.

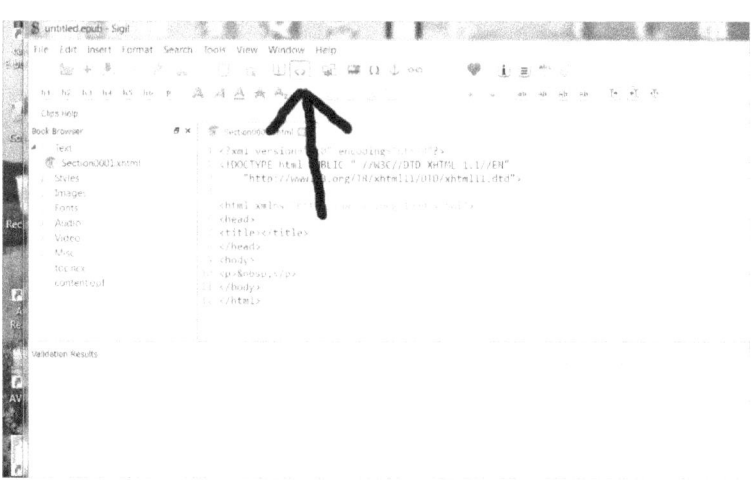

Sigil is an editing program that can be used to create an epub formatted book from start to finish. The arrow above points to the menu item [<>]. This button is highlighted in the above screen shot. The panel that is displayed in this screenshot shows programming code, not the

© Zero Point Healers

actual text of the book. We will use Sigil not to write and edit a book from scratch but to edit an existing epub created from the Calibre conversion.

Now it is time to load the epub formatted book that you created using Calibre. Click on the file menu item on the left of the menu listings at the top.

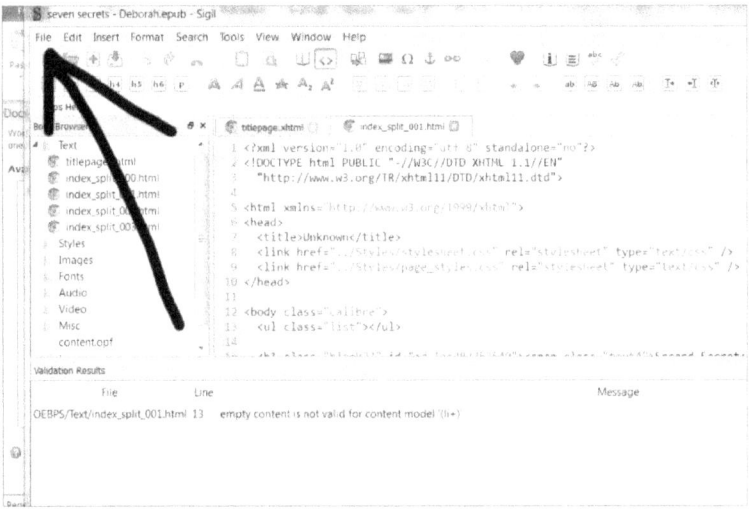

A drop down menu will pop up. Select "open" which is the second choice in the list. This will bring up a new drop down menu that allows you to select the folder on your computer where you stored the epub file formatted using Calibre.

© Zero Point Healers

The folder containing the file you need to open will contain several files. Select the file that is labeled with the $\mathcal{S}$ designation. This is the epub formatted file that was created using Calibre. Other files will be shown in the folder. Ignore those files. When you click on the file with the Sigil designation, a warning screen may appear which reads:

> *This EPUB has HTML files that are not well formatted. Sigil can attempt to automatically fix these files, although this can result in data loss. Do you want to automatically fix the files?*

You have a choice of choosing Yes or No. I always select Yes. In doing so, I have never seen a problem with a loss of content in my books. If you too choose to answer this question with a "yes, it is a good idea to check your book from start to finish to insure that it contains the full content you created originally.

Once you click "yes" to this question your book will be loaded into Sigil. *Opening* the epub book into Sigil takes 10-30 seconds. Look in the bottom left of the screen to track the loading progress before proceeding to the next step.

When loading is finished you can view and edit your book by clicking on the image icon of the open book shown below in the Sigil screenshot.

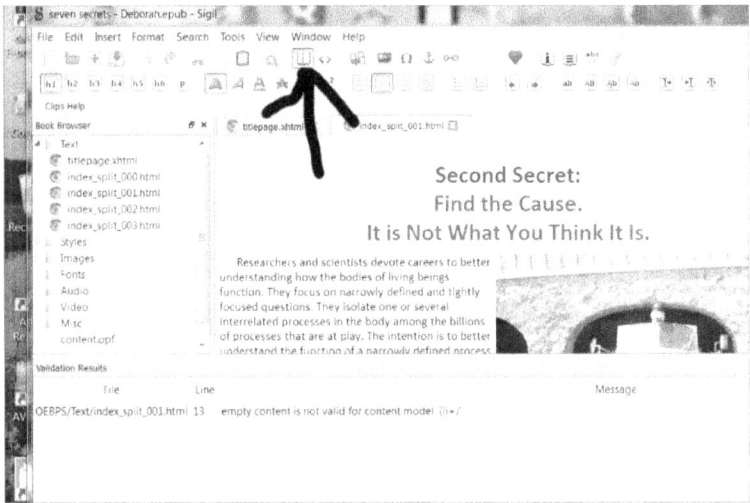

For illustration purposes I have loaded one of my books. Once your own book has been loaded you can now edit it directly in the screen panel just as you would edit your book using Microsoft Word.

Listing of the book sections are found in the column on the left of the page. The first chapters of the book are shown on the screen and are found in the file titled index_spilt_001.html. This file is listed at the top of the screen panel. This

　　　© Zero Point Healers

was the naming of the files in this particular book. The naming of the files in your book will be different.

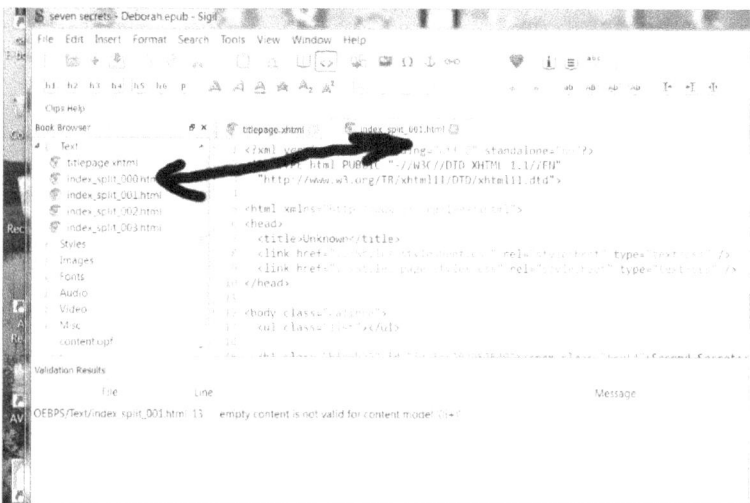

When you click on the file name immediately below titled index_spilt_002.html which is listed in the left column, this same file name will pop up at the top of the screen panel. The section of the book associated with that particular file will automatically be shown in the screen panel.

You can load all chapters of the book by clicking on all of the file names in the left hand column. When this is done, the files associated with the I chapters of your book will be listed at the top of the screen panel. If you want to view a section of your book other than the section that shows on the screen panel, click on a different file name listed at the top. It will turn from gray to white and that content will be displayed show on the screen. .

To view the text of the book (not the programming code) on the main panel make sure to highlight the menu item pictured as the open book. When the open book icon is highlighted the text of the book will be shown in the screen panel. AN example from one of my books is displayed on the next screen shot. You see text, not programming code. I recommend that you examine all pages of your book to insure that the appearance is just the way you want it. Just because it looks great as a paperback book or ebook does not mean that it will look great when read on smart phones such as Androids.

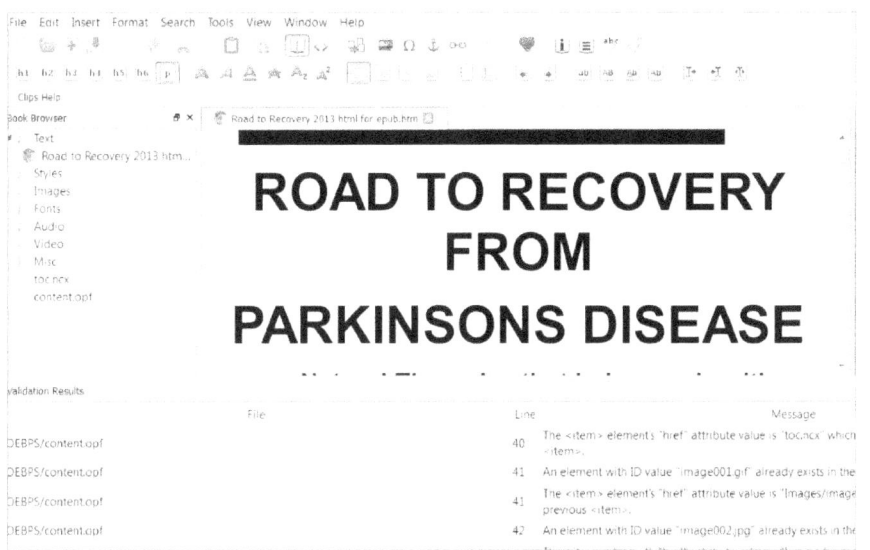

Step Six: How to Find Errors

Now that you have reviewed your epub book, entered your edits and are pleased with how it looks, it is time to check for errors in your epub file. Conversions using Calibre are getting better and better but they are not perfect. Errors are generated in the conversion which will block your book from being accessed by smart phones. You will not even get to first base when trying to list your epub with Google Play if there are errors in your epub file.

© Zero Point Healers

The location of the Flight Crew error checker in Sigil is depicted below in the screen shot by the black arrow at the top of the screen. The arrow is pointing to a Green Check mark (which is the designation for the error checker).

Click on the green check. This will generate a listing of any and all errors that will be shown at the bottom of the screen panel highlighted in pink. The location of errors that are identified by Flight Crew will show up at the bottom of the screen. The location is shown below by the black arrow.

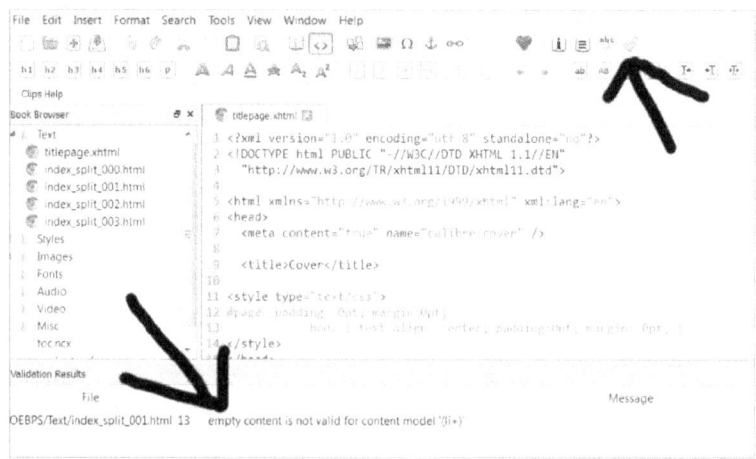

© Zero Point Healers

I ran the error checker and found one error for my most recent book. The error is highlighted in pink at the bottom of the screen. This error must be fixed before the epub will be accepted by Google Play or other internet smart phone download services that will see your books.

Do not be alarmed if the Flight Crew error checker finds a long list of errors in your epub file. All of the errors can be corrected one way or another without too much trouble even if you are a novice at programming.

Step Seven : How to Correct Errors

If you have not already done so,

1. Highlight the menu item to the right of the open book [<>] icon at the top of the panel. This will bring up the programming code for your book.
2. Click on the Green Arrow Flight Crew Error checker (if you have not already done so).
3. Were you lucky and no errors showed up? Proceed to Step Eight.

© Zero Point Healers

4. Did the error checker find errors? You need to correct all of the errors before proceeding to the next step of the conversion process.

The error that was generated in my explained includes three information components: File, Line and Message:

File: OEBPS/Text/index_split_001.html

Line: 13

Message: "empty content is not valid for content model '(li+)'"

Of course each error will be reported differently. How do find the file that is referred to above? The name is clearly listed as

Text/index_split_001.html

Do not worry about OEBPS – all files have this designation. The file listed with the error is listed with all the files in the left column of the page. The arrows in the screen shots below show where to find the file name and where it is listed in the left hand column.

© Zero Point Healers

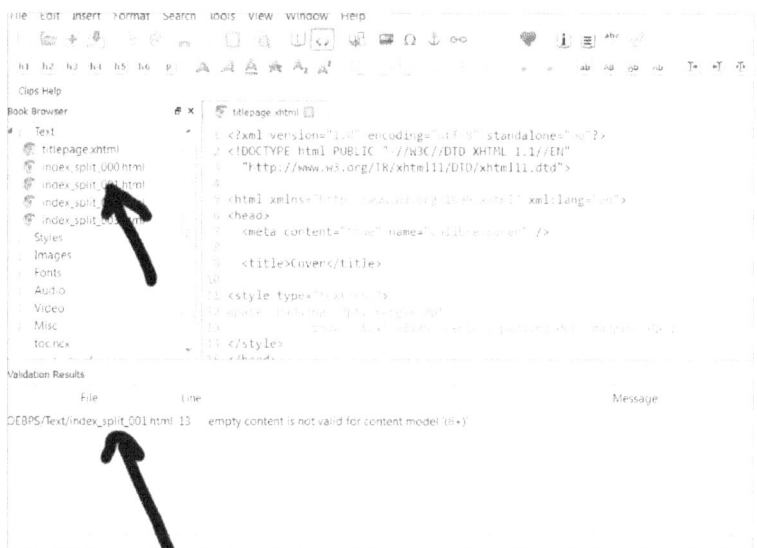

Click on that file name and the file will pop up on the screen panel as shown below.

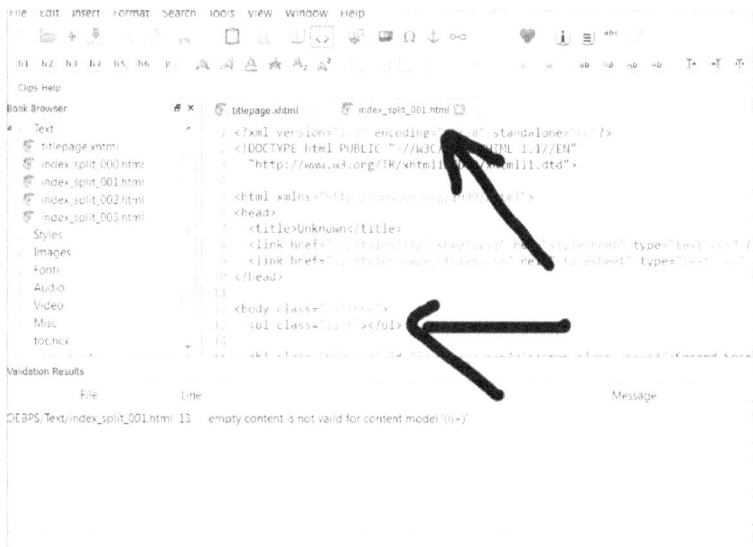

© Zero Point Healers

You can confirm that the programming code that shows on the screen is for the file you need to examine by noting that the file name at the top is not shaded. All of the files that are not shown in the panel are shaded and only one file can appear at a time.

Where is line 13? Notice that there are a series of sequential shaded numbers in a column left of the programming code. These numbers on this screen start with 1 at the top and end with 14 at the bottom. When you grab the slider to the right of the screen these numbers will increase as they are the line numbers associated with each line of programming code.

Here is the code that appeared on line 13:

```
<ul class="list"></ul>
```

Humm ... what in the world does this mean? I am not a programmer, nor do I want to be a programmer! Isn't this all getting a little too complicated?

The answer is no. Most of the fixes to errors are accomplished by deleting the code that is flagged to be in error. I do not know what this code

© Zero Point Healers

means and I do not care, so I simply delete line 13. The deletion is shown below:

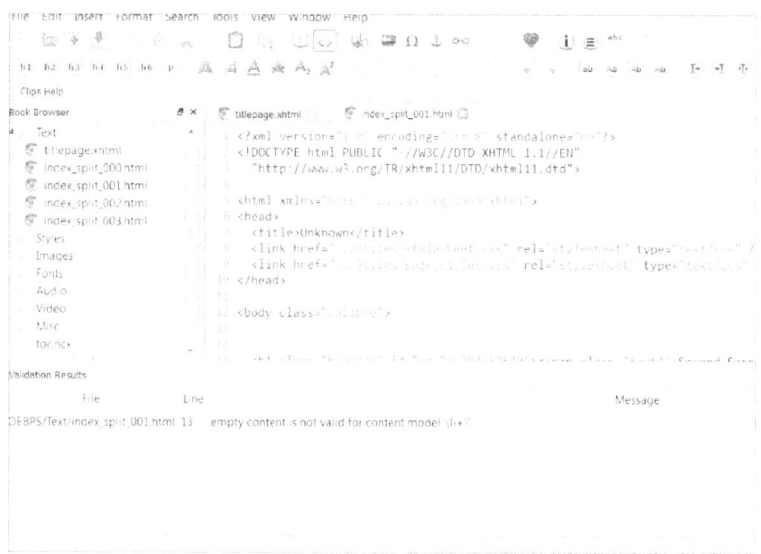

.

Note that everything is the same as before expect line 13 is missing because I deleted it.

OK – did this create garble in the book that people will read on their smart phones? Check it out. Simply click on the open book icon (instead of the programming icon <>which is active) and examine how your book looks. I have now deleted a lot of programming language in my books and guess what? None of the deletions affected how the book looked.

Now, as a matter of routine, save the epubs you alter to new file named in your epub folder on your computer. I simply use the name of the epub and add numbers at the end of the filename. This epub can be saved to Seven Secrets2. Each time I make changes I save the edited files to a newly named file. If I have to go back to a previous file because I messed up the current file there is the most recent backup available.

Now that a change has been made to the files run a new error check on the book to determine if the changes that were made (in this case there was the deletion of one line of code in one line of programming) eliminated the error. When I ran the error checker again, no errors were listed. The deletion did the trick. Deletions are easy and trouble free as are most fixes to the errors that are found.

The process of correcting errors is to read the error message, inspect the programming on the relevant line number, identify the problem from the message and fix the programming code. Sometimes you can delete a small segment of code on a line rather than the entire line. If you are concerned about the impact your deletion has on the book, just inspect the book itself to see if the deletion created any problems.

An error message may ask you to add code to a line. Since you are not a programmer, what do you do with this type of error message?

Here is what I do. I simply copy the message that asks for some change to be entered in the programming code. Then I paste this exact language into a search engine. I also add the word Sigil at the end of the requested search. This is what programmers do to fix their own errors!

Your search will list a number of websites that offer potential fixes. You will always be able to find the solution in someone's website. Know that if you are puzzled by how to eliminate the errors, many other people will be puzzled too and will have already asked and found how to correct the error.

Step Eight: Validate the Epub File

You are probably thinking – wait a minute here.

> *I have already gone to all the trouble to correct whatever errors were found using Flight Crew, the error checker program in Sigil. Why bother to check for errors again using another error checking program? Won't I just be wasting my time? Why bother if no errors were found in the first place?*

The entire purpose of getting an error free epub is so you can post it not only on Google Play but the other services on the internet that make it possible to sell your book to people who want to read it on their phones. Just because you have corrected all the errors flagged in your FlightCrew checks using Sigil (or no errors were found) does not mean that your epub is error free according to the International Digital Publishing Forum.

© Zero Point Healers

International Digital Publishing Forum
Trade and Standards Organization for the Digital Publishing Industry

http://validator.idpf.org

Why should this matter to you? It matters because Google Play and other internet services that sell epubs use IDPF to validate that the epubs submitted to them are free of errors. When you submit your epub to Google Play – they submit it to the International Digital Publishing Forum using the link above. If no errors are found, your epub will be accepted for display on google Play. If errors are found, your epub book will not be accepted and you will not have a clue why it was rejected. You know there were errors, but what errors need to be corrected? Google will not tell you. They will simply reject your epub. You need to validate your epub yourself the very same way google staff will validate it.

After fixing errors using Sigil it is important to submit your epub corrected for all errors you have found thus far to the epub validator. The validator will flag errors not displayed in the messages generated by Flight Crew checker in Sigil.

© Zero Point Healers

Better yet, results from the validator also provide more detailed information about where the errors can be found which are sometimes not shown when using the Flight Crew checker in Sigil.

Click on the IDPF validator link.

http://validator.idpf.org

Then, submit your epub for validation using the link above. You will need to upload the epub file which has the fancy $\mathcal{S}$ associated with the name of your epub file. Errors will be shown on the same page. You need only wait a short time (5-30 seconds). If errors are displayed you will need to return to Sigil to fix all errors that were flagged.

Once you correct the errors using Sigil (usually by deletions) resubmit the file to the validator to verify that the errors have been fixed. Once the validation shows your book is error free (Congratulations!) you are good to go to submit your epub book to Google Play. Do not even bother submitting your epub to Google Play until you are cleared by the Validator to be free of errors.

No, you do not download the IDPF Validation program. You access the IDPF website using the link above and upload your epub from your computer to be validated. Validations are done on the IDPF validation website. It is a good idea to bookmark this website if you are planning on converting a number of books to epubs.

EPUB Validator (beta)

Submit an EPUB document for validation. Your file must be 10MB or less.

Choose File   No file chosen

Validate

About this site

This site uses EpubCheck to provide validation information for EPUB 2 and 3 documents. If you are creating commercial EPUBs in volume, you must install EpubCheck instead of using this site.

Step Nine: Post your Epub book on Google Play

All About Google Play

Most people have not even heard about Google Play. This incidentally gives you an enormous advantage now that you have converted your paperback back to the epub format. Post your epub book now on Google Play. Do not delay. Celebrate the increased visibility this exposure will generate for you.

What is Google Play? It is a digital distribution platform for applications used by Android Smart Phones as well as other smart phones. Think of Google play as a digital media store where you can sell your books to people who prefer to read books on their phones. People who prefer reading books on their phones can browse and download applications developed with the Android SDK and published through Google. Because of its extensive global exposure, Google Play is an ideal outlet which offers your book great exposure. You have gone to all the trouble to write your book. Let Google market it for you!

Access to books offered through Google Play can be offered either free of charge or at a cost you specify. You can place a price on each of your books. Your books are downloaded by readers directly to an Android or Google TV device through the Play Store mobile app, or by

© Zero Point Healers

deploying the application to a device from the Google Play website.

Is it worth your trouble to list your book (now in epub format) on Google Play? You betcha. Google has documented over 50 billion downloads. Some of course are free and others are not. You can obviously sell more downloads of your books to people who want to read them on their phones through Google Play.

Better yet, Google displays a link you provide where a customer can purchase the paperback book. They do not make any money if a customer clicks on this link and purchases your paperback book. Sales of my own paperback books have increased dramatically because of this exposure.

When you post your epub book on Google Play, you do not post any search terms related to the topic of your book. Google has saved the contents of your book and will display your book to the people most interested in reading its content. Now how cool is that?

You can also give permission to allow prospective readers to see 20% of the content which is

© Zero Point Healers

randomly selected. I think this is an excellent way to give prospective readers a preview of the book's contents.

How to Set Up a Google Play Publisher Account

The Google Play website address for uploading your epub books is the following:

https://play.google.com/books/publish

[As an aside – it took me two hours to find the URL address for people like you and I who want to list our books. This may be because the system is new.]

Click on the Google Play link and you will be first taken to the Google sign in page. If you have not signed up for a Google Account you can do so for free on this signup page. Google has a single account now for all programs and services. If you Have Google adwords or adsense or any other google service you already have an email address and password set up.

If you are new to Google you will have to set up a new account. Once your account has been set up (which takes only a few minutes) enter your email address and the password you have set. You will then be taken to the Google Play page where you can list your epub book for sale. A screenshot of Google Play follows so the destination will be familiar when you arrive.

Summary

You are now done! Hooray. I will say this again. I spent two months figuring how to convert my books to epubs but the effort was worth it. Converting books to epubs is not exactly exciting or creative work but it pays off handsomely in the end.

© Zero Point Healers